DEDICATED TO...
YOU!

MR. BEAR GOES TO THERAPY

MAI OTSU

MR. BEAR LIVED IN A TINY FOREST.
THERE WERE LOTS OF OTHER ANIMALS,
BUT MR. BEAR FELT ALONE.

くまさんは小さな森に住んでいました。
他にもたくさんの動物たちがいましたが
くまさんはさびしく感じていました。

MR. BEAR HAD A VERY BIG PROBLEM.
HE DIDN'T KNOW HOW TO TAKE CARE
OF HIMSELF.
EVERY TIME HE FELT SAD, HE HAD AN
URGE TO EAT ANIMALS.

くまさんには、大きなもんだいがありました。
どうやって自分をコントロールしていいかわか
らなかったのです。くまさんは悲しくなると、
他の動物を食べたくなってしまいます。

MR. BEAR KEPT HIMSELF IN HIS CAVE BECAUSE HE DIDN'T WANT TO HURT HIS FRIENDS. BUT, IT MADE MR. BEAR EVEN SADDER.

くまさんは、お友だちをきずつけたくなかったので、どうくつにかくれていました。でも、くまさんは悲しくなるばかりでした。

ONE DAY, HE MET A MASTER IN THE FOREST. HE TOLD MR. BEAR TO TRAVEL FAR FAR AWAY AND LEARN HOW TO

ある日、くまさんは森のししょうに会いました。ししょうは、遠くへ行って自分のコントロールの仕方を学んできなさい、とくまさんに言いました。

ゆけ、むすこよ
"GO, MY SON

SO, MR. BEAR WENT FAR FAR AWAY.
HE FIRST HAD TO PASS A BIG TALL MOUNTAIN.
HE BECAME VERY HUNGRY BUT DIDN'T KNOW
HOW TO GET FOOD AT A NEW PLACE.

そして、くまさんは遠くへ行きました。
まずは高い大きな山をこえなければいけませんでした。
でも、くまさんは食べ物が見つけられなくて、おなかが
空いてしまいました。

THEN HE MET MRS. AND MR. BEARY, THE VERY GREAT FISHERS. THEY TAUGHT MR. BEAR HOW TO CATCH FISH. MR. BEAR FINDS HIMSELF HAPPY WHEN HE THINKS ABOUT FISHING BECAUSE HE CAN FORGET EVERYTHING.

すると、くまさんはつりが上手なくまの夫婦に会いました。2匹はくまさんに魚のつかまえ方を教えてくれました。くまさんはつりをすると、悲しいことを忘れられることに気づきました。

WHEN MR. BEAR WENT DOWN THE MOUNTAIN, HE SAW THIS BEAUTIFUL TOWN WITH LOTS OF RIVERS.

くまさんが山を下ると、そこには川と山がいっぱいあるすてきな町がありました。

THEN HE MET ALLY, THE ALLIGATOR.
SHE IS A VERY KIND ALLIGATOR AND
LOVES HER FRIENDS.

すると、くまさんはワニのアリーに会いました。
アリーは友だちが大好きなやさしいワニでした。

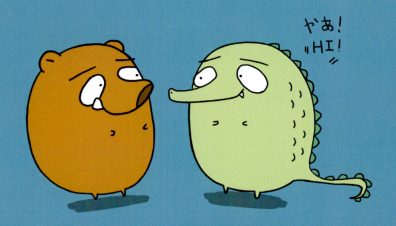

ALLY TAUGHT MR. BEAR HOW TO PLAY CARDS. MR. BEAR LEARNED FROM HER TO SPEND TIME WITH HIS FRIENDS WHEN HE FEELS SAD INSTEAD OF GOING BACK TO HIS CAVE.

アリーはくまさんにトランプを教えてくれました。くまさんは悲しい時はどうくつにもどらずに、友だちとすごすことを学びました。

WHEN MR. BEAR WAS LOOKING FOR A PLACE TO REST, HE MET HUGGY, THE SQUIRREL.

休む所をさがしていると、リスのハギーに会いました。

ハギーはくまさんに大きなハグを
しました。くまさんは幸せで温かい
気持ちになりました。幸せで温かく
なりたい時、くまさんはみんなに
ハグをしました。

HUGGY GAVE MR. BEAR A BIG HUG. IT
MADE MR. BEAR HAPPY AND WARM.
SO, HE GAVE EVERYONE A HUG WHEN HE
WANTS TO FEEL HAPPY AND WARM.

JUMP!

BECAUSE HE WANTED TO LEARN MORE,
MR. BEAR WENT TO ANOTHER TOWN,
BUT HE MISSED HIS FRIENDS SO MUCH.

くまさんはもっと知りたくて他の町に行った
けれど、友だちとわかれて悲しくなって
しまいました。

くまさんはとても悲しくて、友だちから教えてもらったことをぜんぶわすれてしまいました。そして、くまさんは何もかも食べてしまいました。

MR. BEAR WAS SO SAD AND COULDN'T REMEMBER ANYTHING THAT HE LEARNED FROM HIS FRIENDS. SO, HE ATE EVERYTHING.

WHEN HE WAS SAD AND HIDING IN A CAVE,
HE MET MARY, THE VERY LOVING SHEEP.
SHE SAID TO MR. BEAR THAT SOMETIMES WE
GO BACK INTO OLD HABITS, AND IT'S OKAY
BECAUSE IT'S ALSO A PART OF THE PROCESS.

悲しくて、どうくつにかくれて
いると、とても愛情ゆたかな羊
のメアリーに会いました。メアリー
は、これも成長のかていだから
大丈夫、とくまさんに言いました。

MR. BEAR CAME OUT FROM HIS CAVE AND KEPT HIS JOURNEY.
HE WAS BRAVER BECAUSE HE NOW KNOWS IT'S OKAY NO MATTER HOW MANY TIMES HE FALLS. AND...
HE WAS STRONGER BECAUSE HE KNOWS THAT HIS FRIENDS ARE ALWAYS WITH HIM, INSIDE HIS HEART.

くまさんは、どうくつから出てきて、旅を続けました。くまさんは何度失敗しても大丈夫だと知ってゆうきが出ました.そして、、、
くまさんの心の中にはいつも友だちがいると分かって、強く歩いていきました。

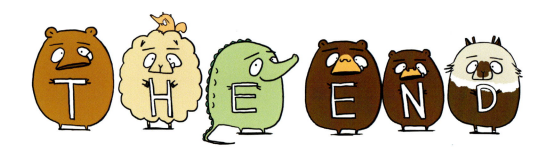

おわり。

Mai Otsu

She lives in Seattle, Washington with two little rats. She was born and raised in Japan and moved to the U.S. to study psychology at the University of Washington.

2匹のネズミと一緒にワシントン州のシアトルに住んでいます。日本で生まれ育ち、ワシントン大学で心理学を勉強するためにアメリカに行きました。

MR.BEAR GOES TO THERAPY

2024 年 5 月 27 日　初版発行

著　　者　　大津 まい

発 行 所　　株式会社　三恵社
　　　　　　〒462-0056 愛知県名古屋市北区中丸町 2-24-1
　　　　　　TEL 052-915-5211　FAX 052-915-5019
　　　　　　URL https://www.sankeisha.com

本書を無断で複写・複製することを禁じます。乱丁・落丁の場合はお取替えいたします。
Ⓒ2024 OTSU Mai　　ISBN 978-4-86693-923-0